The
Love Poems

# of Dr. Willow

"*i lay down and flowers grow*" reprinted with permission from Wake Forest School of Medicine, Winston-Salem, NC, Oasis 2013; issue 28.

Printed in the United States of America
San Bernardino, CA
Kindle Direct Publishing
June 2019

Acknowledgments

I want to thank you dear reader, for the honor and privilege of sharing with you. May these words bring comfort and joy to that place in you that you call home.

I thank Susan Ramundo for page composition and book design, Sabrina Williams for print layout, and Peter Orlando for author photograph and cover design.

Thank you to the Beloved Great Mystery for these musings, I am simply an ear with a pen.

Contents

Beautiful Snowflake

You are a beautiful snowflake
living in a blink of time,

Let us share that time together,
floating thru the air
softly landing
on the branch of a rooted tree,
melting together in the Sun,
and giving drink to our Mother,
finding our way back home.

Snowflakes fall from the sky,
They a part of God
Like you, like me,

Let go of something not belonging,
and turn to Joy,
where there is.

There is no-one else
exactly like you.

My Heart

My heart is an admirable power of light,
able to pierce through the portals of darkness
and shine so brightly that evil runs,
and love enters all who encounter her.

My heart is a singing giant of joy,
for all the tenderness and affection
she bestows and is bestowed upon her.

My heart is a tender rain of sorrow,
for all the suffering and pain,
which cries to her beating womb.

My heart is an open door to God,
who enters steadfastly at her beckoned call,
and whispers sweet love notes in her ear.

My heart is a vessel which the Light fills,
and which emanates into the world.

Sun and Moon

When the Sun and the Moon meet,
they know each another,
in one glance of an eye.

Have faith in true power,
for true power can do,
great things.

The power of the Sun
and the power of the Moon,
create Life on Earth.

When you find that person,
who is the moon to your sun,
and the sun to your moon,

Seize them
and hold on,
dearly and eternally,
for the very turning
of the planet
depends upon it.

When the Sun and the Moon meet,
their ecstatic union
brings forth God.

"*Have Faith*," God says,
for your love ripples
through time and space.

"*Thank you for your light*,"
says the moon to the sun,
says the sun to the moon,

When the Sun and the Moon meet,
Wonders unleash
and skip and twirl across the world.

Recognition

If souls know each other
thru stretches of time,
then surely
we recognize
one another.
Surely we have met
before.

Trust

"Trust in the timing of things,"
The Universe says.
"You see, i will deliver to you right on time."

Healing

My job as a healer,
is to see
that inner light,
that inherent goodness,
no matter how hidden,
how guarded,
how covered,
or confused,
it is there in us all.

When we shine light
on that light,
it expands,
it fills,
it comes out
of its hiding places
with a clarity
that births rainbows.

All we need is for light
to shimmer upon us,
and our natural gifts blossom
and color the world.

i lay down and flowers grow

i am a vessel for the Light, and i am the body of the Earth,
i lay down and flowers grow, i lay down and flowers grow,
because they can, because they do, no thinking, reasoning, worrying,
that is the Nature of things.

Sun & rain, sun & rain, come into me, come into me,
because they can, because they do,
this is the Nature of things.

Purple wildflowers
spontaneously bloom, spontaneously bloom,
as i lay down, as i lay down,
this is the Nature of Life.

i lay down and flowers grow, no pushing, pulling, fighting,
purple wildflowers spontaneously bloom, spontaneously bloom,
for they can, for they do,
from me, my body, the Earth,
as i lay down,
may i lay down.

The Nature of Love

Love knows no direction;
no north, no south, no east, nor west,
no up or down, here or there.
Love knows no bounds.
Love is not practical.
Love is no clock
that can be turned '*on*'
or turned '*off.*'

Love is not reasonable,
Its' intelligence extends beyond reason, far beyond reason.
And so, there is no reasoning with it.

Love does not know distance nor time. It transcends space and time.
You can love someone far away, and whom you may never see again,
that is o.k., that is love.

Love is vast.
Take comfort in the vastness. Fall into this expansive place.
It is peaceful and calm, open and easy,
Embrace it. In acceptance,
you no longer suffer.
Your tenderness, your affection,
they are real.
And they are natural,
a natural part of some continuum.

There is no need for denial, or pain,
there is no use instigating rules,
on something so all encompassing.

Relax in the immensity,
Exhale into the infinity,
Smile,
You are thriving,
for you are choosing love.

This is the Way.
This is the Nature of Love.

Tailspin

i do not know why
he has to throw his gaze
at me like that,
for those brief seconds
that carry me to eternity.
they throw me
into a tailspin;
a nosedive;
a spinning free fall
and i know not where i am
going to land.
i am left spinning for days.
just when i thought i had
all of my composure together.

Daughter

My love for you is so
wide and deep,
like a bowl for you to always rest in.
Remember this, my dear,
a bowl for you to rest in.
You wish for your space,
to run wild and free,
as all young ladies need,
which all young ladies
should be given.

May you be free to move
and breathe, and be the
vitality whom you are,
without confinement or constriction,
but with the safety of
your guardian angels.

Compassion

Be tender with yourself, be tender.
And in that tenderness the gates to our hearts may open.
Imagine them standing wide open.
Compassion helps them to melt.
Melt away all that pain and all that suffering.

I am sorry for the harm that was cast upon you;
the hardship, the agony,
the injustice, the pain.
The mud on your bright beautiful petal which
was so colorful in the radiant sun.
I am sorry for the darkness which came your way.
You do not deserve it.
You do not need it.
It is not you.

You are a beautiful gem who will once again shine.
I have heard your cries and I am here.
Compassion is here.
Compassion has always been a part of you.
You can go on living, and you will be, only,
all the more beautiful.

Every Moment

Every moment,
Life asks,
Will you choose me?

Each moment,
God asks,
are you letting me in?

Certainty

Things unfold as they do,
Without any certainty.
All you can be is certain
of yourself.

River Speak

"*i am so shy,*" i said to the River.
and the River moved quickly,
Singing across the Rocks,
Reflecting the Light of the Sun.
"*you just keep moving,*"
The River said to me,
"*Singing from the rocks in your path,*
Reflecting the Light of the Sun."

Reconciliation

In the quiet
of these low clouds
cushioning our Mother Earth,
let us settle things,
as the snow gently falls.
Remember you and i
are here to love one another
and this great big World.
Without our togetherness
How can we possibly fight
the larger and more important
battles?

I am not a fighter
anyway,
but a lover who wishes
for all to love.

Motherhood

As soon as your child
lets go
of your hand,
That is when
you begin
to pray.

The mother is the one who invites
the guardian angels to intervene.

Blessed Be the Flowers

Blessed be the flowers
who manage to grow in the gravel.
They did not ask to be planted there,
yet grow,
as directed by Life.

Green stems emerging from tiny pebbles,
This is simply where they find themselves,
to be.

Currency

The heart
needs a current of love
to keep on beating.

Love
keeps us alive.
How could we move without it?

In love,
you need no wine or petty things,
no chocolate or TV shows.
You wish to keep
your best clothes on.

In the Midwest,
people have cows,
and know that grass
is no greener on the other side.

The Good Mother

The Universe awakened me
to life, the present moment,
and her mystery of how
she directs us all on our paths.

Like a good mother
who knows
we are self-motivated to do
what we are passionate to do.

And who watches,
listens,
and gently guides us
when she sees we
need someone to
take our hand.

The Deer

In love, do not hold back.
Be the deer jumping over the fence.

True Love

I don't know too much about love,
only that we can fail it,
but it never fails you.
There are moments
when love is close
and your heart is a carol of birdsong.
Moments of
proliferated possibility.

Give your heart permission to love.
True love will
never leave you
and
True love will always find you.

In love,
grant freedom,
never hold
any hostages.

Truth

The truth is
all any of us
ever want, is
love and acceptance,
love and acceptance.

Our souls will seek it
like a man lost in
the desert for water,
tirelessly, endlessly,
never ceasing to hope.

But the truth is
you don't have to travel far,
not even at all,

for this love and acceptance,
love and acceptance,
is right inside of you.

Leap towards it
in the Almighty You.

i saw my soul

i saw my soul
hovering atop the air in the green valley,
Wings beating faster than my heart,
she suddenly dived down to land
on the bare branch of a tree.

One never knows how the magic will take form,
how the planting of a mother
will reach her daughter,
how the wishes of a child,
will blossom into rainforests.

And it is thus a woman
thinks as she does each task,
as she plants each berry,
*"this is for my daughter,
i do this for my daughter."*

"We have so much and we are so blessed,"
she muses from time to time,
beginning with the sun rising,
and ending with the set.
"Light be around, be around"
she beseeches from time to time,
as she builds a little oasis
of fresh fruits and flowers.

i saw my soul
hovering atop the air in the green valley,
finding nectar in a flower,
the planting of a mother
always reaches her daughter.

God Said

i asked God,
"if i should do this, please give me a sign,"
and God said,
"what more do you want?
isn't it sign enough that you thought it?"

Bliss

Our natural state is bliss,
I am being breathed.
Return, return,
to this natural state
of bliss.

Bliss nature is life worth living.

Live in your bliss nature,
dwell in your bliss blood.

Our natural state is bliss,
You are being breathed.

Ananda, Ananda, Ananda,
Being content with what is,

Thankful for all your blessings,
Counting our blessings,
this is Bliss.

Unlimited Possibility

Unlimited possibility can casually
stroll in like nothing out of the ordinary,
a nonchalance in her gaze.

She may greet you in the morning
before the sun has even risen,
letting you hold her soft fur against
your own naked skin.

Unlimited possibility may make
herself as comfortable as she can,
facing an open window with
cool air blowing in,
after eating strawberries
from the kitchen counter.

Life is uncertain,
but, life is also,
unlimited.

Circles

There is a part of me,
who has always known
a part of you,
who has always loved you.

If the Universe moves in circles,
Then, it must be how
Our lives dance,
how they keep dancing.

Rooms in our Hearts

We have more rooms in our hearts
than we know,
Some we are no longer using or
some we are not taking care of very well,
but, they are bigger than we know.

We have plenty of space for visitors,
plenty of rooms to offer them for their stay,
Perhaps some of those rooms are unfinished,
perhaps many are dusty and in disarray;
but then again,
it is o.k., for
we are all simply becoming persons,
simply becoming human beings.

"*i am here to love*," i remind myself,
each day,
in my ordinary tasks,
my little hum-drum days,
it guides me.
As i speak to people, Listen to people.

It was my heart falling

It was my heart falling
with a plop on the floor,
colorful wings splayed wide,
tiny and bewildered and
trapped in a space
not easy to fly out of.

It was my heart falling
and the cat picked it up,
the beautiful cat with
green eyes and black and white hair,
a moment's gaze
into each other's soul.

It was my heart falling,
without warning,
crashing and plunking down on the floor,

the cat took it in,
and my heart did not leave
but glowed even brighter,
a beacon of light.

The Path

At times the path is
bumpy ice or goopy mud,
not easy to walk,
but we walk just the same,
because we are alive,
because our bodies are built to.

At times the path is
bumpy ice or goopy mud,
we debate whether to go,
but we need the clouds,
as we need the sunshine.

At times the path is
slippery ice or sloppy mud,
Appreciate the easy days,
appreciate the hard days,
Just stop and rest as you need.

Magic

In the tiniest corners
and murkiest moments,
Magic awaits
ready to leap out
in an instant
in one considerate word,
in one loving gesture,
Magic awaits.
Magic is here, magic is there,
present and available.

The moments which take your breath away
are magical moments,
the invisible web
suddenly made visible.

In the tiniest corners and
murkiest moments,
Magic awaits,
when i see you in me,
and you see me in you.

Love

Love is simple,
we need not complicate it.
Listen when someone
tenderly speaks,
Smile when you gaze
into the eyes of the ones you love.

Is love ever lost?

Is love ever lost
or does it merely float on
up into the breeze,
to land somewhere with the dawn,
carried by bees or birds,
and finding another lap
to rest upon.

Me

Me?
A piece of a puzzle
hoping to find her way
into the right box
for a chance
to fit in
somewhere
and
make a
beautiful
picture.

Suffering connects our hearts

Suffering connects our hearts,
for we forget the
unimportant differences,
in our quest for solace.

Suffering connects our hearts,
our hearts open wide,
stretching out long tendrils,
to softly reach one another,
like the roots of white aspen trees,
who know they are One.

Raise your sword of Light,
and Step out with Faith
into your day,
your life,
your world.

Son

Forever lighting my heart,
Forever knowing my ways,
When you laugh,
My heart laughs with you,
When you cry,
My heart cries too.

A heart grown
From the Earth herself,
Could be no bigger.

When your heart shines,
the dark night
is bright once again.

We Begin with Long Hair

We begin with long hair
and long ideas,
which fall out
or are cut shorter by the years.

Remember our innocence?
remember our dreams?

Now it is our children
who carry this flag.
Can we provide them with sturdy shoes
to make it?

May our children find
their fairy book castles
and treasures of gold.
Their fair maidens and strong knights.
Their lives of value and fortune,
of legacy and honor.
Of purpose and passion.
Of happiness, hope, and joy.

Success in your eyes
may be different from mine.
But we are all such simple
and pitiful creatures,
I can tell by your eyes,
and you can tell by mine,
if we have achieved it

LIFE IS MESSY

Life is messy,
Sticky with blood, sweat, and tears,
And crud in her eyes.
Sometimes tacky rather than pleasing,
Impolite, with the manners of a tantruming child,
or gummy with wind and salt in her hair.
Her toes may smell in the shoes she walks in,
She may stumble and fall,
And pick herself back up again.

Life sheds in the house,
Hairs that get caught in furnaces and pipes
and the bottoms of the legs of chairs.
She coughs up,
With clogged breathing tubes,
Spattering, sometimes over steering wheels
And horns which honk.

Life is messy,
Even though we try to clean up around the edges, and
Weed out the long dead stems,
Each time a new seed is planted, life grows again.

Life is messy,
And we have to sweep up the crumbs on the floors of our hearts,
And find a place to throw them,
We have to wipe the jackhammers from our ears and
wash away our sorrows in the shower, or out in the rain,
or in a hot spring bubbling from our mother.

But sometimes fires burn a little too long or a little too far,
or dirt lines forgotten on abandoned floors,
and we need to wipe away the gray film on the windows of our souls,
So we call in help,
To wipe clean what they can,
To shake out the carpet and roll it back out again looking new,

The Sages see what lay within the fabric.

We call them to replace old lenses itchy and smeared,
And spread balms onto spilled surfaces,
We call them when our voices are no longer sure and strong,
but scratched and uneven,
and there are envelopes left piled on our desks.

We all do what best we can, even they.
Knowing that messes move places and change forms,
but remain somewheres,
Until the Earth herself swallows, making her, her own.

We may try to prevent illness and disease the best we can, however,
life is messy,
and sometimes we find cockroaches in the bathroom
of the best restaurants
in town, or
ticks embedded in our own bodies.
We are only, after all, human.

Teachings from Knitting

Even if you have never done it before,
begin, and it will turn out fine.

You can always stretch it to make it meet.

To every front side,
there is a backside.

If the colors do not match perfectly,
it will make it all the more beautiful.

Holes can be mended easily.

It is easier than you think,
once you sit down to do it.

There is more than one tool that will work.

Find a nice spot to sit.

Just tie the loose ends together.

Life is forgiving. Especially, fuzzy yarn.

Flip it around so you can work comfortably and confidently.
Stop when you are tired,
Only do it while it is fun.

Shape it around the strongest.

Take a candy break and look out the window.

Find the largest thread and use it.

If you can't see, feel.

Just be yourself, this is success.

Hope

Hope greets me each morning
in black letters
on the back of a folded paper,
written on top of faded ink.

Hope greets me in cursive
by my ten-year-old daughter
who leaves her pencil laying next to it,
as if waiting to write the next sentence.

Hope greets me upon the window ledge
above the kitchen table
for all of us to see,
as we breakfast.

Find a place to sail

Yes life is uncertain
and life is unfair
How 'bout looking round girl
You'll see it everywhere

Find a place to sail girl
Find a place to sail
Life is so uncertain
When you lift her
pretty veil

Find a lake to sail on
where water flows real fine
find a place to glide girl
there is always time

Life is only rocky
when you take the
bumpy road
Find another route girl
See where that path goes

If you float on sunshine
despite the bitter winds
If you sail in bubbles
when rain is crashing in

Darkness hides in corners
around each pretty wall
How come god says evil
must live with us at all?

Find a place to sail girl,
find a place to sail,
Life is so uncertain
when you lift her pretty veil,

Life is only rocky
when you take the bumpy road,
Find another route girl
Let that path unfold.

Water

Water, Water
Flowing, Knowing,
Circling Up,
Snowing Down.

Frozen Crystals
Growing, Knowing,

Light and Sound.

In Stillness,
A Gift is Found.

Call it Gold

When you find the trees do not
bear gold leaves which you once sought,
then look above into the sky
to see the changes passing by.

The monkey's tail has faded fast
simple thoughts will never last
He swiftly grows into a man
Racing faster than he can
a once cherished land.

He no longer is content
To roam not fearing time ill-spent,
without seeking in relent
the capture of the fresh green scent.

When you have what you hold
know enough to call it gold,
Naked branches are not bare,
You can see the sky from there.

Still Life

And when I turn inside
from the world that is cold
to see the still life
in my barren abode
I am warm, for I know
in the world that is cold
A man who is warm
gives this life with his rose.

I Call it Mango

Seagulls cry
I close my eyes
to see the music man

Miles away
Forever plays
because I know he can

Guitar strings
Forever bring
a scarecrow to my home

Looking back
at railroad tracks
I know I'm not alone.

About the Author

Born Carolyn K. Williams in Evanston, Illinois USA in 1965, the writer and counselor known as Dr. Willow (short for Dr. Williams-Orlando) listens to soul speak and the voices of Mystery. You may find her at water's edge or perhaps laying under the moon.

Visit www.mountainvoicehealth.com

Made in the USA
Las Vegas, NV
23 September 2023

77997324R00038